Animals Can Sing

by M.O. Lufkin

Illustrated by Saptarshi Nandy

Animals Can Sing

1. I went__ to the for-est and list-ened for a sound.   I heard a swarm of bum-ble-bees
2. (I) went a lit-tle fur-ther and list-ened for a cry.   And there__ was a wolf__ pup
3. (I) went a lit-tle fur-ther to see what I could see.   I saw a la-zy bull-frog
4. (I) thought__ I was lost and I let__ out a scream.   And who heard but a hun-gry bear

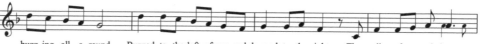

buzz-ing all a-round.   Buzzed to the left of me, and buzzed to the right.   Then all of a sud-den,__
howl-ing at the sky.   Howled to the left of me, and howled to the right.   Then all of a sud-den,__
look-ing right at me.   Croaked to the left of me, and croaked to the right.   Then all of a sud-den, the
fish-ing in a stream!   Growled to the left of me, and growled to the right.   Then all of a sud-den, he

|1.2.3.| |4.|
(spoken)   (spoken)

they buzzed out of sight! Bzzzzz!   I   Grrrrr! 5. I came in-to a mea-dow and looked at ev-'ry-thing. The
he howled out of sight! Aroooo!   I
frog jumped out of sight! Ribbit!   I
rum-bled out of sight!

(spoken)

an-i-mals came clos-er and they start-ed to sing!   The bees all buzzed! Bzzz!   The wolf pup howled! Arooo! The

bull-frog croaked! Rib bit! The hun-gry bear growled! Grrr! 6. I ran from the mea-dow and all its wild_sounds. I

ran be-tween the an-i-mals and dodged them all a-round.   Ran to the left of them, and

ran to the right.   Then all of a sud-den,   I was out of sight!

Published in the United States by Literary Mango, Inc.

Little Neck, New York. First edition, 2017.

www.literarymango.com

Author: M.O. Lufkin

Illustrator: Saptarshi Nandy

Editor: Jody Mullen

Summary: Illustrations and text take the reader on an adventure into a mystical forest to discover bees, a wolf, a frog and a bear. The story is written in rhyme with an accompanying song.

Paperback ISBN 978-1-946844-06-4

Hardcover ISBN 978-1-946844-07-1

I went to the forest and listened for a sound
I heard a swarm of bumblebees buzzing all around

Buzzed to the left of me, and buzzed to the right
Then all of a sudden, they buzzed out of sight!

Bzzzzzzzzzzzzzzzzzzzzzzzzzzzzzzzzzzzzzzzzzzzzzzzz!

I went a little further and listened for a cry
And there was a wolf pup howling at the sky

Howled to the left of me, and howled to the right
Then all of a sudden, he howled out of sight!

Arooooooooooooooooooooo!

I went a little further to see what I could see
I saw a lazy bullfrog looking right at me

Croaked to the left of me, and croaked to the right
Then all of a sudden, the frog jumped out of sight!

I thought I was lost and I let out a scream
And who heard but a hungry bear, fishing in a stream!

Growled to the left of me, and growled to the right
Then all of a sudden, he rumbled out of sight!

Grrrrrrrrrrrrrrrrrrrrrrrrrrrrrr!

I came into a meadow and looked at everything
The animals came closer and they started to sing!

The bees all buzzed

Bzzzzzzzzzzzzzzzzzzzzzzzzzzzzz!

The wolf pup howled

Arooooooooooooooooooooooooooo!

The bullfrog croaked
Ribbit!

The hungry bear growled

Grrrrrrrrrrrrrrrrrrrrrrrrrrr!

I ran from the meadow and all its wild sounds
I ran between the animals and dodged them all around

Ran to the left of them, and ran to the right
Then all of a sudden, I was out of sight!

Try These Children's Books

Thinking of Mom by MO Lufkin is a heartfelt story about loss. Mom takes care of Ella every day. But when Mom is overcome with illness, Ella is left feeling sad, angry, and helpless and doesn't know how to deal with those emotions. Dad helps Ella to call on the good memories of Mom to help her feel happy again. Children coping with loss and the grown-ups who love them will find comfort in this engaging and empathetic story told alongside beautiful watercolor images.

In *Start With Sorry* by P.T. Finch, Three-year-old Luna loves to spend time with her older brother, Asher, and she wants to do everything he does. But when they sit down to draw pictures together, Luna feels upset that she can't do everything he can do. When she reacts in anger, Asher is sad and doesn't want to color with her anymore. With Mommy's help, Luna learns how to make amends for hurting her brother's feelings. Kids love this story, and adults appreciate the valuable lesson it teaches about empathy for others.

Buddy's New Friend is P.T. Finch's second children's picture book in a series about siblings Luna and Asher. Their pet cat, Buddy is lonely during the day when everyone is away at school and work, so the family goes to a local animal shelter to find him a new friend. In addition to curing Buddy's loneliness, the siblings learn a valuable lesson in empathy when they choose an older dog among swarms of cute puppies. Will Buddy and his new friend get along, or will they fight like cats and dogs? Read the book to find out!

www.literarymango.com

Literary Mango